THE PRINCIPLES OF DEMOCRACY

WHAT IS INDIVIDUAL FREEDOM?

JOSHUA TURNER

PowerKiDS press

New York

Published in 2020 by The Rosen Publishing Group, Inc.
29 East 21st Street, New York, NY 10010

Copyright © 2020 by The Rosen Publishing Group, Inc.

All rights reserved. No part of this book may be reproduced in any form without
permission in writing from the publisher, except by a reviewer.

First Edition

Editor: Melissa Raé Shofner
Book Design: Reann Nye

Photo Credits: Seriest art Bplanet/Shutterstock.com; cover Hill Street Studios/
DigitalVision/Getty Images; p. 5 https://commons.wikimedia.org/wiki/File:Scene_
at_the_Signing_of_the_Constitution_of_the_United_States.jpg; p. 7 Dean Drobot/
Shutterstock.com; p. 9 Tanarch/Shutterstock.com; p. 10 FatCamera /E+/Getty
Images; p. 11 Jacob Lund/Shutterstock.com; p. 13 Jessica Kourkounis/Getty Images
News/Getty Images; p. 15 Simon Ritzmann/Photodisc/Getty Images; p. 17
Matthias Clamer/Stone/Getty Images; p. 19 Blend Images - Hill Street Studios/
Brand X Pictures/Getty Images; p. 21 JGI/Tom Grill/Blend Images/Getty Images;
p. 22 Monkey Business Images/Shutterstock.com.

Cataloging-in-Publication Data

Names: Turner, Joshua.
Title: What is individual freedom? / Joshua Turner.
Description: New York : PowerKids Press, 2020. | Series: The principles of
democracy | Includes glossary and index.
Identifiers: ISBN 9781538342763 (pbk.) | ISBN 9781538342787 (library
bound) | ISBN 9781538342770 (6 pack)
Subjects: LCSH: Liberty–Juvenile literature. | Democracy–United States–Juvenile
literature.
Classification: LCC JC599.U5 T87 2019 | DDC 323.440973–dc23

Manufactured in the United States of America

CPSIA Compliance Information: Batch #CSPK19: For Further Information contact Rosen Publishing, New York, New York at 1-800-237-9932

CONTENTS

★ ★ ★ ★ ★ ★ ★ ★ ★ ★

WHAT DOES IT MEAN TO BE FREE?.... 4

KNOWING YOU'RE FREE............ 6

INDIVIDUAL FREEDOM
AND DEMOCRACY................ 8

FREEDOM IN EVERYDAY LIFE 10

INDIVIDUAL AND
GROUP FREEDOMS 12

FREEDOM, FAIRNESS,
AND EQUALITY 14

TOO MUCH FREEDOM? 16

FREEDOM FROM ACTIONS 18

FREEDOM TO ACT 20

THE IMPORTANCE OF
INDIVIDUAL FREEDOM 22

GLOSSARY 23

INDEX 24

WEBSITES 24

WHAT DOES IT MEAN TO BE FREE?

The United States was founded on the idea that individual freedom is one of the most important features a society can have. For the Founding Fathers, freedom meant they would have the ability to vote and **worship** how they chose.

For abolitionists, or the people who wanted to end slavery, it meant giving these rights to African Americans. For **suffragettes**, it meant giving these rights to women. Freedom in the United States means being able to exercise your rights in society.

THE SPIRIT OF DEMOCRACY

The first society to give individual freedom to citizens by allowing them to vote in elections was ancient Greece. The Greeks believed the government should decide what freedoms people would have and then **protect** them.

The Founding Fathers believed individuals should be able to make their own choices about how to live their lives.

KNOWING YOU'RE FREE

Freedom doesn't mean being able to do whatever you like. We have rules and laws that all citizens are expected to follow, such as not stealing or lying.

Freedom means being able to make choices about your own life. You can decide what to eat or what to read. You can choose what to study in school and what job you want later in life. One of the most important freedoms in the United States is the freedom of speech, which lets you **express** yourself without being **censored**.

In a free society, people can study what they want in college and decide for themselves how they'll **contribute** to society.

INDIVIDUAL FREEDOM AND DEMOCRACY

Democracy is important for individual freedom, and it starts with voting. In a free society, people get to choose their leaders in free, fair, and open elections. The person you vote for might not always win. But if you voted, you still had a say in the election.

In the United States, the government is chosen by the people. This means the U.S. government must protect the individual freedoms of the people or lawmakers face being voted out of office.

THE SPIRIT OF DEMOCRACY

The Enlightenment was a period of European history in which famous thinkers thought deeply about the world around them. It claimed that democracy and individual freedom were important for citizens to live well and be happy.

American democracy has worked for over 200 years because it promises its citizens certain individual freedoms.

FREEDOM IN EVERYDAY LIFE

★★★★★★★★★★

Individual freedom can take many meanings in everyday life. It can mean big things, such as getting to vote for the president of the United States. It can also mean little things, such as choosing what clothes you'll wear each day.

Making good choices becomes even more important when you have more freedom. This is because the more freedom you have, the more **responsibility** for your actions you have as well. You can choose to eat healthy foods, or not. It's up to you.

> The more freedom an individual has, the more important making good choices, such as helping out others, becomes.

INDIVIDUAL AND GROUP FREEDOMS

Just as individuals have freedoms, groups of people have freedoms, too. For example, in U.S. elections there are two parties: the Democrats and the Republicans. Each party is a group made up of many individuals.

Each party has the freedom to decide who they want to represent it. Then, as a group, all Americans get to choose the president. You may not always be in the majority, but everyone gets a say in a democracy.

THE SPIRIT OF DEMOCRACY

In 2008, Barack Obama won the **nomination** of the Democratic Party and went on to be elected president. Many people thought he would lose the election. It was because of each person's individual freedom to choose that he won.

Political **conventions** are a great way for individuals to come together as a group. There, they may exercise their freedom and choose who they want to represent, or speak for, them in government.

FREEDOM, FAIRNESS, AND EQUALITY

✭✭✭✭✭✭✭✭✭

Is everyone equally free? Is freedom always fair? These questions aren't easy to answer, and they may have different meanings for different people.

Individual freedom in a democracy means everyone has an equal and fair amount of freedom. Each person's vote counts once. And each person has the freedom to cast his or her vote. To have real freedom, you must have fairness from others. You must also share that freedom equally with others.

Freedom of speech means that even if you don't like what someone is saying, they have a fair and equal right to say it, just as you do.

TOO MUCH FREEDOM?

In a democratic society that allows for individual freedoms, people are given the tools, such as an education, to make good choices. However, the responsibility to make good choices is in the hands of each person. This is why someone might choose to get in a fight rather than talk about his or her problems.

Some people think U.S. citizens have too much freedom. As long as you aren't breaking the law or hurting others, freedom means having the right to make your own decisions.

THE SPIRIT OF DEMOCRACY

The Cold War between the United States and the Soviet Union was a battle of ideas between **liberal** democracy and **communism.** The United States fought for individual freedom and eventually won in the early 1990s.

In the American Old West, there was not yet a strong government authority to make people follow the law. This is why it was called the "Wild West."

17

FREEDOM FROM ACTIONS

There are two different kinds of individual freedom people in society have. The first is the freedom from the actions of others. Because of the laws of our country, people have freedom from others stealing their property or from trying to harm them.

The police and the government protect these freedoms. The people who are in charge are elected freely and fairly. This helps to make sure that an individual's freedom from others is protected by society as a whole.

> Police and elected officials help protect people's freedom from the actions of others.

FREEDOM TO ACT

★ ★ ★ ★ ★ ★ ★ ★ ★ ★ ★

The second kind of individual freedom is the freedom to perform actions. This could mean deciding what you want to eat for breakfast or where you want to work.

A person's freedom to act has limits. Their actions must not hurt others or take away another's freedoms. In a democratic society, nobody has the right to take away the freedom of another person. A person's freedom to act and make choices about his or her life is what individual rights are all about.

★ ★ ★ ★ ★ ★ ★ ★ ★ ★

THE SPIRIT OF DEMOCRACY

Today, the United States fights against **terrorist** groups around the world in hopes of protecting people's individual freedoms. The world is a better place when more people are safe from harm and able to choose their own paths in life.

★ ★ ★ ★ ★ ★ ★ ★ ★ ★

The freedom of an individual to choose his or her own path in life is key in a democratic society.

THE IMPORTANCE OF INDIVIDUAL FREEDOM

Individual freedom is at the heart of any democratic society, including the United States. Without individual freedom, the United States wouldn't exist. This is because individual freedom is the basis of democracy.

Individual freedom allows people to make their own choices. But the freedom to choose comes with a lot of responsibility. This is why every person should try to use his or her individual freedom to do the right and good thing. Remember that your freedoms are only protected until you harm the freedoms of others.

GLOSSARY

censor: To remove things that are thought to be harmful to society.

communism: A way of organizing a society in which the government owns the things that are used to make and transport products and there is no privately owned property.

contribute: To give something, such as money, goods, or time, to help a person, group, or cause.

convention: A large meeting of people who share similar work or interests.

express: To talk or write about something that you are thinking or feeling.

liberal: Not opposed to new ideas or ways of behaving that are not widely accepted.

nomination: The act of choosing someone for a job, position, or office.

protect: To keep safe.

responsibility: Something you should do because it is morally right or legally required.

suffragette: A woman who worked to get voting rights for women in the past when women were not allowed to vote.

terrorist: A person who uses violence to scare people as a way of achieving a political goal.

worship: To show respect and love for a god especially by praying or having religious services.

23

INDEX

A
abolitionists, 4
actions, 18, 20

C
censorship, 6

E
elections, 8, 12
equality, 14

F
Founding Fathers, 4
freedom of speech, 6

L
laws, 6, 16, 18

P
parties, 12
police, 18

R
responsibility, 10, 16, 22

S
slavery, 4
suffragettes, 4

V
voting, 8, 10, 14

W
women, 4

WEBSITES

Due to the changing nature of Internet links, PowerKids Press has developed an online list of websites related to the subject of this book. This site is updated regularly. Please use this link to access the list: www.powerkidslinks.com/pofd/ind

24